D1498008

ENDANGERED ANIMALS

SALAMANDERS

McLEAN MERCER REGIONAL **LIBRARY**
BOX 505
RIVERDALE, ND 58565

BY KRISTEN POPE

Published by The Child's World®
1980 Lookout Drive • Mankato, MN 56003-1705
800-599-READ • www.childsworld.com

Acknowledgments
The Child's World®: Mary Berendes, Publishing Director
Red Line Editorial: Editorial direction and production
The Design Lab: Design
Amnet: Production

Design Element: Shutterstock Images
Photographs ©: Sebastian Kennerknecht/Minden Pictures/
Corbis, cover, 1; Shutterstock Images, 4, 11, 22; John
Cleckler/U.S. Fish and Wildlife Service, 6–7; Teal
Waterstrat/U.S. Fish and Wildlife Service, 8; Patrick
Gijsbers/iStockphoto, 10; iStockphoto, 12; Billy Hustace/
Corbis, 15; Chris Caris/U.S. Fish and Wildlife Service,
16; Gary Peeples/U.S. Fish and Wildlife Service, 17;
Shawn Milar/U.S. Fish and Wildlife Service, 18–19; Matt
Jeppson/Shutterstock Images, 20–21

Copyright © 2016 by The Child's World®
All rights reserved. No part of this book may be reproduced
or utilized in any form or by any means without written
permission from the publisher.

ISBN 9781631439711
LCCN 2014959641

Printed in the United States of America
Mankato, MN
July, 2015
PA02264

ABOUT THE AUTHOR

Kristen Pope is a writer and editor with years of experience working in national and state parks and museums. She has taught people of all ages about science and the environment, including coaxing reluctant insect lovers to pet Madagascar hissing cockroaches.

TABLE OF CONTENTS

CHAPTER ONE

A WORLD OF SALAMANDERS   4

CHAPTER TWO

THREATS TO SALAMANDERS   11

CHAPTER THREE

PEOPLE ARE HELPING   16

What You Can Do, 22

Glossary, 23

To Learn More, 24

Index, 24

A WORLD OF SALAMANDERS

Salamanders live in wet, wooded areas.

A smooth, wet face pops out of a pond in the woods. It is the face of a salamander. It looks for a moist, dark place on land. It may even find a slug or worm to eat. This little salamander is not alone. There are more than 600 species of salamanders in the world. But more than half of them face extinction.

WARNING SIGNS

Many salamanders, such as the red-spotted newt, are brightly colored. These salamanders are poisonous. The bright colors tell other animals to stay away. They are a warning that these salamanders have bad-tasting liquids in their bodies. The bright colors keep salamanders from becoming another animal's food.

Salamanders are amphibians. Some types of salamanders are called newts. Most salamanders look like a cross between a frog and a lizard. They have smooth, moist skin like frogs. But they have long tails like lizards. Salamanders have four short legs. Their bellies drag on the ground. Some species spend most of their time in water. They use gills to breathe. Others are born with gills, but lose them as they grow. They develop lungs to breathe. Still others do not have gills or lungs at all. Instead, they breathe through their skin. They are called lungless salamanders.

Some salamanders live in shady areas in the forest. They stay out of the sun. The sun could dry out their moist skin. They often live under rocks and logs or in trees. They may dig burrows into the earth. Other salamanders spend their whole lives in the water. Sixteen species of salamanders never see the sun. They live in completely dark caves.

Salamanders eat worms, slugs, and snails. Some larger species might also eat fish and mice. Sometimes, they sneak up and grab their food quickly. Other times, they wait until food passes to snag it. A few species can even catch food with their tongues.

The largest salamander in the world is the Chinese giant salamander. It can grow to be 6 feet (1.8 m) long.

This California tiger salamander has short legs and smooth, moist skin.

These salamander eggs will eventually turn into salamander larvae.

The smallest species lives in Mexico. It grows up to 0.6 inches (1.5 cm) long. Most species do not grow larger than 6 inches (15.2 cm). The heaviest giant salamanders can weigh 140 pounds (63.5 kg). But most salamanders weigh less than 1 pound (0.5 kg).

Nearly all salamanders hatch from eggs. Many are born in water, though some hatch on land. Larvae emerge from the eggs. These larvae do not look like adult salamanders. Unlike adults, the larvae have fins and gills. The larvae live in water.

They turn into salamanders in three to six months. After that, many species move to land. They live in other animals' old burrows. Most stay close to the ponds where they were born. Some salamanders can live up to 55 years. But most live for about ten years.

The United States has more species of salamanders than any other country. More than 50 species live in the Appalachian Mountain range alone. The California tiger salamander lives on the West Coast of the United States.

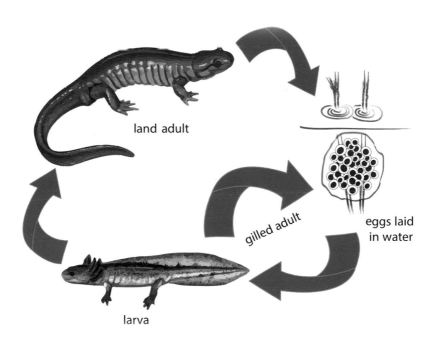

land adult

eggs laid
in water

gilled adult

larva

Salamanders go through different phases throughout their lives.

Adults are 7 to 8 inches (17.8 to 20.3 cm) long. They have yellow markings around their mouths. These markings make it look as though they are always smiling.

There are many species of salamanders in the world. But their numbers are falling. Many salamander species are endangered. They may become extinct if people do not try to help them.

Without human help, some salamander species may go extinct.

CHAPTER TWO

THREATS TO SALAMANDERS

Salamanders have been on Earth for millions of years.

Salamanders have been on Earth for more than 160 million years. Today many face extinction. Some species are already extinct.

About half of the salamander species in the world are threatened. There are 130 to 150 species of salamanders

Some salamanders must cross roads to find food and lay eggs.

in the United States. More than 40 percent of them
are threatened or endangered. When an animal is
endangered or threatened, special laws often protect it.

Humans are the biggest threat to the world's
salamanders. Around 95 percent of salamander
habitat is threatened in California because of human
activities. People put buildings and farms on land where
salamanders live. People also cut down forest trees. When

these trees are cut down, there is less shade in the forest. The forest floor becomes hotter and drier. It is then difficult for salamanders to stay moist and cool.

Humans using vehicles and building roads can hurt salamanders, too. People have built roads through salamander habitat. The roads block salamanders from getting the things they need. They may cut off a path to a pond where a salamander finds food. They may also block a salamander from the area where it lays its eggs. Sometimes salamanders cross roads. Many are killed by cars.

Human-made oils, chemicals, and sewage threaten salamanders, too. They damage salamander habitat. They can soak into a salamander's skin. This can kill it or cause health problems.

FISHING BAIT

Some people catch wild salamanders to use as fishing bait. Many salamanders die this way. Using salamanders as bait spreads disease. Disease spreads faster when affected salamanders move from one area to another. This may happen when people use salamanders as bait in areas other than where they found the salamanders.

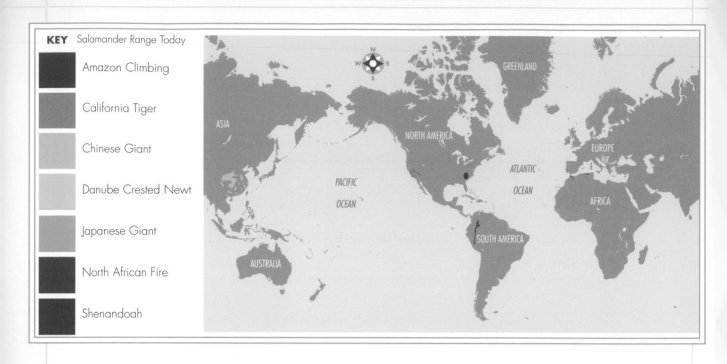

KEY Salamander Range Today

Amazon Climbing

California Tiger

Chinese Giant

Danube Crested Newt

Japanese Giant

North African Fire

Shenandoah

This map shows seven of the more than 600 species of salamanders found in the world.

Millions of wild amphibians are caught in the United States each year. They are sold as pets, including many salamanders. In some parts of Asia, salamanders are sold as key-chain pets. The fire-bellied newt is sold sealed in a plastic package connected to a key chain. It lives in the sealed key chain for a few weeks. Then it dies because it does not have food or water.

Some people in Asian countries eat salamander as a special treat. The Chinese giant salamander and Japanese giant salamander were nearly hunted to extinction.

Many of the world's salamander species face extinction. People around the world are working together to try to save them.

Chinese giant salamanders are at risk of becoming extinct.

CHAPTER THREE

PEOPLE ARE HELPING

Scientists are helping this Santa Cruz long-toed salamander larva.

Governments and international groups work together to protect endangered species, including salamanders. International laws protect salamanders and their habitats. Governments and groups build tunnels to let salamanders safely cross roads. Signs warn drivers that salamanders

Scientists study salamanders, such as this hellbender, to help protect them.

may be present. People care for the streams and wet areas where salamanders live. These efforts help the number of salamanders grow.

LAWS TO PROTECT SALAMANDERS

In 2009, the California tiger salamander was given special protection. Lawmakers put it on the California Endangered, Species List. It is a list of protected species. The list protects other amphibians, as well as birds, mammals, fish, and reptiles. In January 2015, there were 152 species of animals on the list.

Scientists also help salamanders. They study these animals to learn more about them. Some move threatened and endangered salamanders to safer places. Later they bring the salamanders back to the wild. Other scientists study how people help or harm salamanders. They have discovered that people can sometimes carry diseases to salamanders by accident. People walk into salamander habitats with muddy shoes on. The mud can carry salamander

These scientists are studying a cleaned-up pond that is now salamander habitat.

diseases. Scientists also teach people about salamanders at museums, schools, and nature centers. People learn how to protect these animals.

There are many different types of salamanders. But if people do not work to protect them, there may be fewer in the future. That is why scientists, governments, and other groups work to protect the world's salamanders.

Salamanders of all colors, such as this red salamander, can be saved with help from humans.

WHAT YOU CAN DO

- If you see a salamander in the wild, look but do not touch. The oils and salts on your skin can harm the amphibians.

- Never keep salamanders as pets.

- Do not use salamanders as fishing bait.

- Tell people all about salamanders. Tell your friends and family and encourage them to learn more, too.

GLOSSARY

amphibians (am-FIB-ee-unz) Amphibians are cold-blooded animals that begin life in the water, and many move to land as an adult. Salamanders are amphibians.

endangered (en-DANE-jurd) An endangered animal is in danger of becoming extinct. Many salamander species are endangered.

extinction (ek-STINK-shun) Extinction happens when all animals in a species die out. Some salamander species face extinction.

gills (GILZ) Gills are body parts that fish and some salamanders use to breathe in the water. Some salamanders lose their gills and grow lungs.

habitat (HAB-uh-tat) A habitat is a place in nature where animals or plants live. Forests, ponds, and caves are salamander habitats.

larvae (LAR-vee) Larvae are young salamanders or insects just hatched from their eggs. Larvae hatch from salamander eggs.

species (SPEE-sheez) A species is a group of animals that are similar and can produce young together. There are more than 600 species of salamanders.

threatened (THRET-und) A species that is threatened is likely to become an endangered species. Some salamander species are now threatened.

23

TO LEARN MORE

BOOKS

Berger, Melvin and Gilda. *Amphibians*. New York: Scholastic, 2011.

Borgert-Spaniol, Megan. *Salamanders*. Minneapolis: Bellwether, 2012.

Hesper, Sam. *Fire Salamanders*. New York: PowerKids Press, 2015.

WEB SITES

Visit our Web site for links about salamanders:
childsworld.com/links

Note to Parents, Teachers, and Librarians: We routinely verify our Web links to make sure they are safe and active sites. So encourage your readers to check them out!

INDEX

behavior, 4, 5

California Endangered Species List, 17
California tiger salamander, 9, 17
Chinese giant salamander, 6, 15

diseases, 13, 18–20

fire-bellied newt, 14
food, 4, 6, 13, 14

habitat, 5–6, 9, 12–13, 16, 18

Japanese giant salamander, 15

larvae, 8–9
laws protecting salamanders, 12, 16–17

Mexico, 8

red-spotted newt, 5

United States, 9, 12

McLEAN MERCER REGIONAL LIBRARY
BOX 505
RIVERDALE, ND 58565